Discovering
Cultures

Poland

Sharon Gordon

BENCHMARK BOOKS

MARSHALL CAVENDISH
NEW YORK

With thanks to Dr. John S. Micgiel, Director, East Central European Center, Columbia University, for the careful review of this manuscript.

Benchmark Books
Marshall Cavendish
99 White Plains Road
Tarrytown, New York 10591-9001
www.marshallcavendish.com

Library of Congress Cataloging-in-Publication Data

Gordon, Sharon.
Poland / by Sharon Gordon.
p. cm. — (Discovering cultures)
Summary: An introduction to the geography, history, people, and culture of Poland.
Includes bibliographical references and index.
ISBN 0-7614-1724-9
1. Poland—Juvenile literature. [1. Poland.] I. Title. II. Series.
DK4147.G67 2003
943.8—dc22

2003019101

Photo Research by Candlepants Incorporated
Cover Photo: Zbigniew Jablonski/Envision Stock Photo

The photographs in this book are used by permission and through the courtesy of; © 2003, Tina Manley, All Rights Reserved: 1, 24, 27, back cover. Walter Bibikow/Danita Delimont.com: 4, 6, 15, 31, 32, 42 (top). Getty Images: V.C.L., 7, Raymond Gehman/National Geographic Society, 9, Steven Weinberg, 22, 33, 42 (bottom). Corbis: Dave G. Houser, 8, 43 (right); Steve Raymer, 14, 18, 19; Bettmann, 16, 44 (right); Jose Fuste Raga, 20; Raymond Gehman, 23, 28; James Marshall, 26; David Turnley, 36; Pawel Libera, 38; Archivo Iconographico S.A., 44 (left). Mark Downey /Lucid Images: 10. The Image Works: Hideo Haga, 12–13, 37; Skjold, 30; UPPA/Topham, 45. Polish National Tourism Office: 34–35.

Map and illustrations by Ian Warpole
Book design by Virginia Pope

Printed in China
1 3 5 6 4 2

Turn the Pages...

Where in the World Is Poland?

The Republic of Poland is in central Europe. On a map, it looks a little like a square. Its northern border stretches 277 miles (446 kilometers) along the Baltic Sea. Germany is on its western border. Lithuania and Russia are on the northeast. To the east are Belarus and the Ukraine. Beyond the mountains on Poland's southern border are Slovakia and the Czech Republic.

Poland's Carpathian Mountains

4

Map of Poland

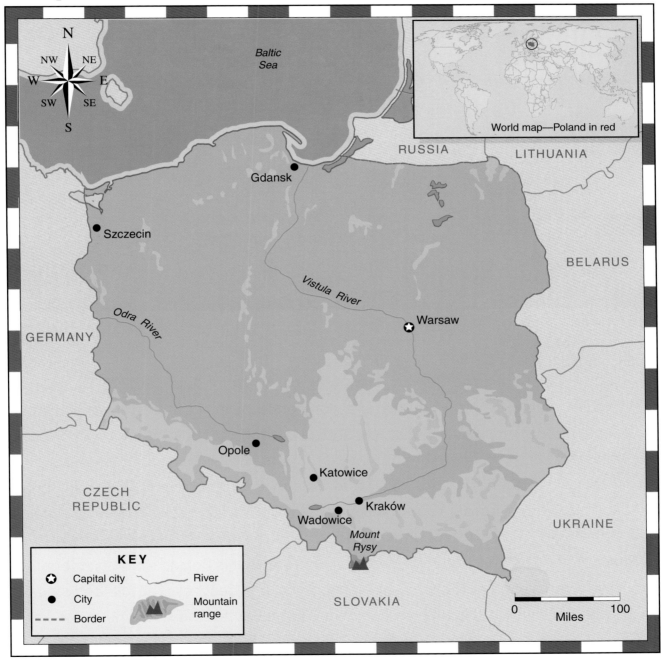

Baltic Sea

N
NW NE
W E
SW SE
S

World map—Poland in red

RUSSIA
LITHUANIA

● Gdansk

● Szczecin

BELARUS

Vistula River

Odra River

GERMANY

☆ Warsaw

● Opole

● Katowice

● Kraków

Wadowice

Mount Rysy

CZECH REPUBLIC

UKRAINE

SLOVAKIA

KEY

☆ Capital city
● City
--- Border

～ River
⛰ Mountain range

0   Miles   100

A Polish farming village

Poland is about the size of New Mexico. Most of this 120,725-square-mile (312,683-square-kilometer) country is a flat, *fertile* plain. In fact, the name Poland means "land of fields." The Polish lowlands are good for growing crops, but not for keeping enemies out. There are no rivers or mountains on the east or west. So it has been easy for other countries to invade Poland throughout its 1,000-year history. Poland's southern border is protected by the Sudety and Carpathian mountains. They are part of a larger mountain range called the Alps. Mount Rysy, in the High Tatras Mountains, reaches 8,199 feet (2,499 meters). It is Poland's highest mountain.

Along Poland's northern coast is a strip of sunny beaches. They lie between the two harbor cities of Gdansk and Szczecin. Southeast of the coastline is the Lakes Region. This area is filled with forests and over 7,000 lakes. Many of the lakes are

Warsaw, the capital of Poland

connected by small rivers or *canals*. Vacationers and tourists like to sail, camp, and fish along these waterways.

Below the Lakes Region is the Central Plains. This area is covered with thousands of farms that produce beets, rye, potatoes, and sugar. Many of Poland's major cities are also on the plains, including Warsaw, the capital. The Vistula River, Poland's longest river, crosses the Central Plains. It flows 675 miles (1,086 km) from the Carpathian Mountains to the Baltic Sea.

The Polish Uplands in the south are an area of rolling hills and high mountain peaks. Like the Central Plains, this area is also good for farming. Potatoes and wheat are grown here. Minerals such as coal, copper, lead, and zinc are mined in the Uplands. Opole, a city in the Uplands along the Odra River, is known for its cement industry.

Wawel Castle and Cathedral on the Vistula River

Kraków is one of Poland's oldest and most charming cities. It is at the foothills of the Carpathian Mountains. Kraków was one of the few Polish cities that was not destroyed during World War II. Many old castles and historic churches still stand on the narrow cobblestone streets in some neighborhoods. One such area is Wawel Hill, on the banks of the Vistula River. The Wawel Castle and Cathedral are said to have been built over the cave of the legendary Wawel Dragon. This monster was defeated by a brave shoemaker named Krak, after whom the city was named.

Just outside of Kraków is the Wieliczka Mine. For over a thousand years its deep tunnels and caves have produced Polish salt. Miners have their own underground volleyball and tennis courts, a health clinic, and even a chapel made entirely out of salt! Part of the mine is open to tourists. After seeing the mine, they can eat at the world's deepest restaurant, over 410 feet (125 m) underground. The Wieliczka Mine is visited by nearly 800,000 tourists each year.

Bialowieski National Park

Bialowieski National Park is Poland's oldest national park. At 26,255 acres, the park contains the last of the original forests that once filled Europe. The area was set aside as a *reserve* in 1921 and as a national park in 1932. The park is part of the Bialowieza Primeval Forest, a large woodland near the Russian border. This area dates back to 8,000 B.C. The forest is made up of huge trees that are hundreds of years old. It also has many rare animals and plants. The last of the European bison still roam here, as well as a rare breed of horses called tarpans. A visit to the Bialowieski National Park is like taking a walk back in time.

9

What Makes Poland Polish?

A proud Polish veteran

Polish people, also known as Poles, are proud and patriotic. They love their country and everything that is Polish, from food to music. Through the darkest days, Polish people have kept a sense of humor. They like to laugh, and enjoy hearing a funny story or joke.

During World War II, Poland came under the control of the German Nazis and the Russian Communists. For several years, Poles lost their freedom.

This caused them to grow stronger and more united as a people. Today adults tell their children about the war to help them appreciate their freedom. Poles can never forget the *concentration camps* that were built by the Nazis. Thousands of visitors come to Poland each year to visit Auschwitz. One of the largest concentration camps was located there. One and a half million Jews, Poles, Gypsies, and Soviet prisoners of war were killed in the Auschwitz camp.

People living in Poland have a lot in common. Almost everyone speaks Polish. They also share the same religion. Nearly 95 percent of Polish people are Roman Catholic. Their religion helped to keep Poles together even when they were ruled by other nations. Each Sunday, all work stops and Polish families get dressed up to go to church. In Polish homes, it is

A Roman Catholic church

common to see statues or pictures of Jesus and the Virgin Mary.

Poland has given the world many great musicians. Frédéric Chopin, who lived in the early 1800s, wrote the music for many formal dances, called polonaises. In these graceful dances, couples walk around the dance floor with their heads held high. The polonaise became the musical symbol of Poland. Chopin also wrote many mazurkas, which came from Polish folk dances. Mazurka dancers click their heels and stomp their feet as they twirl around the dance floor. Polka music is another kind of popular Polish music. It is enjoyed in Poland as well as

Polish couples enjoy a lively dance.

Street musicians in traditional dress

in other countries, such as the United States. This lively dance music is often played on the accordion.

Poland's writers and poets have won many Nobel Prizes. These artists helped to keep the Polish spirit alive during difficult times. Over the years, many talented Poles had to leave their country in order to make a living. Roman Polanski, a Polish actor and movie director, left his homeland after his mother died in the Nazi concentration camps. He came to America and made many successful movies. His 2002 movie, *The Pianist*, received three Academy Awards.

Polish folk art includes wood carvings.

Polish people are known for their beautiful crafts and folk art. These traditions have been handed down for generations in the country towns and villages of Poland. They make beautiful woven tablecloths, rugs, and wall hangings. Lovely lace patterns are crocheted by hand. Wood carving, pottery, and glass painting are also popular. Poles are known for their colorful painted designs on boxes and wooden spoons. Cepelia stores are shops that carry Polish folk art throughout the country.

Once upon a time, people thought the sun moved around the earth. In the late 1500s, the great Polish scientist Nicolaus Copernicus studied the planets and discovered just the opposite! He saw that the earth and all the other planets actually move, or revolve, around the sun. But at the time, this view went against the teachings of the Catholic Church. For many years, Copernicus had to keep this knowledge a secret. He was afraid he would be punished. When he was almost

A painting of Nicolaus Copernicus

seventy years old, he finally agreed to publish his discovery. Eventually, his work was accepted. Copernicus became known as The Father of Astronomy.

Poland and the United States share a common war hero. Tadeusz Kosciuszko went to the Royal Military School in Warsaw to become a soldier. He came to America in 1776 and volunteered to fight for independence with the colonies. He also designed the fortress at West Point Military Academy in New York State. As a reward for his help, he was given U.S. citizenship. The Kosciuszko Bridge in New York City is named after this freedom-loving Polish soldier.

Today, Polish soldiers and soldiers from the United States work together on military missions. Poland is proud to be an *ally* of the U.S. in the North Atlantic Treaty Organization (NATO). This military *pact* has guarded Europe since the end of World War II.

Wycinanki

One of the most famous Polish crafts is *wycinanki*,
or paper cutouts. It started in the mid-1800s and has
become a favorite folk art tradition. Poles scrub and paint
their walls in the spring. Then they decorate them with
handmade cutouts shaped like flowers, roosters, or hearts.
They use layers of different colors to create unique designs.
Wycinanki is also popular with tourists. As times change,
adults hope young people will not lose interest in this
traditional folk art. They hope they will continue
making the cutouts with their children
and grandchildren.

Living in Poland

In general, Poland is a crowded country. More and more people have moved from the country to the cities to find work. This has created a housing shortage in the cities. More than half of all Polish families live in apartment buildings that were built after the war. Although there is still not enough room, Poles try to make the best of it. Sometimes relatives live together in order to get a bigger apartment. Often, neighborhood apartments have a common area for children to play. They do not have to go far to find friends.

Crowded apartments in a Polish suburb

The most popular Polish meals include thick soups and meat dishes. Poles start their day with *sniadanie*, an early breakfast. This meal might include bread and butter with sausage or cheese. Around noon, people usually eat a sandwich. A large meal, called the *obiad*, is eaten in the early evening. This may be eaten between

A row of new townhouses

3:00 P.M. and 5:00 P.M. A fourth meal of the day, *kolacja*, can also be large, or it may be just a cup of tea and a roll.

Until recently, not many Polish families had a car. Today, those that do have small cars because the price of gas is very high. But that does not mean

Poland's roads are empty. Trucks and buses fill the city streets. Farmers drive their tractors and work carts down country roads. Family members lead their animals along. Neighbors walk down the street to visit each other. Driving down a road in Poland can be quite an adventure—*Uwazaj!* (Watch out!)

In the past, most Poles believed that mothers should stay home to raise the children. Today, Poland is not a wealthy nation. Most families struggle to make ends meet. More and more, both mothers and fathers must work to support the children.

About one-third of Poles work in factories that

A busy Polish street

A woman making blue jeans in a factory

produce steel, glass, chemicals, and cloth. Others mine Poland's many natural resources, such as lead, copper, and nickel. The coal mines near Katowice are among the largest in the world. Fishing is another important industry. Cod, herring, and hake are taken from the Atlantic Ocean.

Poland's countryside is filled with beautiful farms. Farmers grow crops such as rye and potatoes. Many farmers still plow their fields with horses instead of tractors. In the hilly areas of the south, sheep are raised for wool, and cattle for milk and meat. Hog farms are also found throughout the country.

Farmers plow their field.

Poland will become a member of the European Union (EU) in 2004. The EU is a group of western European nations that work together on issues of money, science, and politics. As Poland becomes more involved in the world economy, workers hope there will be new markets for their products and that new jobs will be created. A better economy will allow factories and farms to update their equipment.

A street vendor sells flowers.

Polish people love flowers. Street vendors set up their businesses everywhere. Workers stop at the local flower shop on their way home. Apartment balconies are often decorated with cheerful flower boxes. Sometimes, neighbors choose to share their gardens so they can grow more kinds of flowers and plants.

To the millions of Polish-speaking people around the world, their language seems quite normal. But to the rest, the Polish language may look difficult to learn. Polish has thirty-two alphabet letters. That is six more than the English alphabet. To someone who does not speak Polish, the words look like a bunch of jumbled letters. But some things are easy to understand. In Polish, the last name of a man ends in the letter "i." A woman's last name ends in "a." So if a boy's last name is Skiwenski, his sister's last name would be Skiwenska.

Let's Eat!
Kielbasa Maple Bites

Kielbasa is a type of smoked, spicy Polish sausage, usually made from pork. Ask an adult to help you prepare this recipe.

Ingredients:

12 ounces kielbasa

2 tablespoons Dijon mustard

1/4 cup maple syrup

Salt and pepper to taste

Wash your hands. Cut kielbasa into bite-size pieces. Mix the mustard and maple syrup together. Dip sausage pieces into the mustard mixture. Push the kielbasa onto metal sticks called skewers and grill over medium heat. Cook for about three minutes per side or until browned and heated through. Makes six servings.

School Days

Polish schoolchildren on a field trip

One hundred years ago, only the rich attended schools in Poland. Poor people did not have the opportunity to get an education. But during the 1900s, a better educational system was started. By the 1980s, almost 98 percent of the population could read and write. Today, that number is near 100 percent.

Education is taken very seriously in Poland. It is free and schools are open for all children. About half the children between ages three and six attend kindergarten. But all children must attend school, called *szkola*, from ages seven through fourteen. The school year begins on September 1 and ends in mid-to-late June. The children have a two-week break in winter, as well as Christmas and Easter vacations. The school day begins around 8:00 A.M. The day ends for younger students around 1:00 P.M. and older students stay till about 2:30 P.M. There are no school uniforms.

Sharing a book in the classroom

Until September 1999, all Polish children attended eight years of primary school, and then a secondary school if they chose. But Poland's system of education is changing once again. Now a student in Poland goes to primary school from ages seven to thirteen. Then from ages thirteen to sixteen, they attend a lower secondary school, called *gimnazjum* (gymnasium). Children in secondary school are graded by the numbers one to six, from "excellent" to "fail."

After gymnasium, a student can attend a two-, three-, or four-year program at various kinds of schools. Some may choose a vocational school. There they might learn a special skill like woodworking or computer science. Others attend a preparatory school called a lyceum. There they can study subjects they will need for college.

Polish students study subjects such as history, religion, and science. Today, there is a great effort to teach children English, as well as other European languages. While the Communists ruled Poland, only Russian was allowed to be taught. Now, Poland is trying to make up for lost time. Teachers have been

Two students study plants in school.

brought in from other nations to teach English. Poland's children need to know this language if they want to work in international companies.

After secondary school, the students take a maturity examination. If they pass, they can enter a college or university. Poland has many public and private universities, some of which are very old. The Jagiellonian University in Kraków was founded in 1364.

Over the last few years, many more Polish students have chosen to go to college. They see it as a way to better jobs. People with college degrees do not have a problem finding work in Poland.

The Witch and the Angels

At recess, schoolchildren in Poland like to go outside and play games with their friends. One popular game is called the Witch and the Angels. The witch marks out a prison area on one side of the playground. A "home" is made for the angels on the opposite side. When the angels leave their home, the witch tries to catch them. If an angel is caught, it is brought into the witch's prison. The angel can be rescued if touched by another angel. The angels like being safe in their home. They sing:

One, two, three,
the witch is looking at me.

Four, five, six,
she knows a lot of tricks.

Seven, eight, nine,
on us she'd like to dine.

She'll throw us to the stars,
so, quick, let's run afar!

Just for Fun

Polish people work hard all week, including Saturdays. But Sunday is a day of rest. After church in the morning, families enjoy a Sunday lunch together. Afterward, Polish families and neighbors may take a walk or relax in the local park. Children ride their bikes with friends. Those in apartments relax on their balconies and talk with neighbors.

Children in Poland enjoy playing games and sports. Soccer is popular. Large crowds cheer on professional teams in the city stadiums. Polish children also enjoy volleyball, field and ice hockey, and basketball. "Streetball" is similar to basketball, but with fewer players and only one hoop.

The High Tatras Mountains provide plenty of year-round activity for Poles and tourists.

Polish boys ride a double bicycle in Kraków.

30

Rafting on one of Poland's many rivers

In the spring and summer, hikers take to the trails to see the beautiful mountains. In the winter, the Tatras are popular with skiers. One of the best ski resorts in Europe is Zakopane, which is Poland's highest town.

One of children's favorite activities in the summer is camping. Families find a clearing in a forest and set up a tent and a campfire. They go swimming in a nearby lake or hike up a mountain. Some camping grounds have huts with running water and electricity for those who do not want to "rough it."

Almost all Poles love to fish, especially in the late summer months. Poland's many lakes and mountain streams are favorite spots to fish.

A castle in the Carpathian Mountains

Poland's beautiful castles are popular with both Poles and visitors. Many have been turned into museums. At Wawel Castle in Kraków, visitors can see ancient weapons, including a sharp sword that was used to crown a new king. In May, music lovers visit Lancut Castle, in the Carpathian foothills, to hear famous musicians play.

Polish people also enjoy watching television. Many Poles are purchasing satellite dishes so they can see programs that are made in western Europe and the United States. Polish radio is also popular for listening to the news and other programs.

Horses

For hundreds of years, Poland has loved its horses. It is famous for its excellent horse farms and horse *breeding* stables. Polish Arabian horses are especially prized. The Janow Podlaski farm in eastern Poland has sold its horses to rich and famous people around the world.

In the past, only the wealthy could afford horseback riding. Today, it is a sport enjoyed by many Poles. Some stables rent rooms to visitors who stay to ride. Beginning riders can receive riding instructions. More advanced riders can learn how to jump with their horses. Young children enjoy Hucul ponies. These small, friendly animals come from the Polish mountains. Those who are afraid to get up on a horse can take a ride in a horse-driven carriage.

Let's Celebrate!

Children in Poland celebrate their *imieniny* (name day), instead of their *urodziny* (birthday). Almost all Polish children are named after saints or important kings from the past. Name days are a special time for families to get together for dinner. They bring flowers, gifts, or chocolates. They wish each other "*Wszystkiego najlepszego*! (All the best!)"

Christmas is the most popular religious holiday in Poland. Churches throughout the country put up Nativity *creches* that show Mary, Joseph, and the baby Jesus. In Kraków, special tin creches called *szopka* are shaped like the church of Saint Mary. Skilled artists enter their handmade creches in a competition. After the winner is announced, all the creches are put on display throughout the holiday season.

Christmas caroling is also popular in Poland. Many carols are hundreds of years old and were written by Polish peasants. These songs could be

Polish Christmas carolers

Santa Claus stops for a picture.

sad, funny, or happy. Beautiful religious carols were written by Catholic monks. Some popular carols set the Christmas story in a Polish village instead of Bethlehem.

Christmas Eve is called *wigilia*. On Christmas Eve day, families fast. This means they eat nothing until the first evening star appears in the sky. Then they begin their celebration with a huge feast of twelve different dishes, one for each month of the year. Generally fish is served, such as herring or pike, with potato dumplings, cabbage, and delicious desserts. Families sing hymns and open their Christmas presents. Then the whole family goes to Christmas Eve Mass. They often go to church again on Christmas Day and then return to their homes for another delicious meal.

Polish weddings are important celebrations. Wedding guests may wear traditional clothing, such as a beautifully embroidered vest. After the church ceremony, family and friends join the couple at a feast with delicious foods, like roast duck and goose. An old tradition is that the parents greet the new couple with salt, bread, and wine. This shows their wish that the couple will

Girls in traditional dress

never go hungry or thirsty. The reception is a happy event with lots of dancing. Sometimes, the dancing lasts all night long. In the morning, the guests put a special cap on the bride's head. This shows that it is time for her to leave her family and join her husband in a new life.

Candles on the soldiers' graves

After a long, cold Polish winter, everyone looks forward to the first day of spring. Some villages celebrate with parades and parties. Polish adults and children enjoy celebrating the end of winter by drowning the Marzanna. This small straw scarecrow is a symbol of winter. Sometimes, schoolchildren will march down to a local river and throw the Marzanna into the water. They shout, "*Do widzenia zimo!* (Goodbye winter!)" and "*Witaj wiosno!* (Welcome spring!)"

Not all Polish holidays are happy ones. September 1 is a very sad and serious day in Polish history. It is the day when Germany's Nazi leader, Adolph Hitler, sent troops into Poland at the opening of World War II. September 1 is also the first day of school in Poland. Schoolchildren remember this day by putting fresh flowers on the graves and statues of those who tried to stop the invasion.

Wet Monday

In Poland, the day after Easter is called Wet Monday. This holiday celebrates a tradition that started in the Middle Ages. Back then, the water baptism of Prince Mieszko, on the Monday after Easter, united all of Poland under Christianity. But, over the years, the holiday became a day of practical jokes. The boys would get up very early in the morning and throw buckets of water on the girls. The girls would get their revenge on the boys the next day. Today, both boys and girls soak each other on Monday—and hope they can find some dry clothes to wear afterward!

The flag of Poland is made up of two horizontal bands. The white one on top symbolizes freedom. The red one below represents the blood of those who died for Poland's freedom.

Poland's main unit of currency is the zloty. It can be divided into 100 groszy. It is expected that Poland will join the European Union in 2004, and the European Monetary Union (EMU) in 2007. The zloty would then be replaced by the euro.

Count in Polish

English	Polish	Say it like this:
one	jeden	YEH-den
two	dwa	d-VAH
three	trzy	TCHEE
four	cztery	ch-TER-ee
five	piec	pee-YINCH
six	szesc	SCHESCHT
seven	siedem	SHED-em
eight	osiem	OWSH-em
nine	dziewiec	JEV-yinch
ten	dziesiec	JESH-inch

Glossary

ally A friend or military partner.

breed To keep and raise animals.

canal A waterway dug across the land.

concentration camp A place where prisoners of war are kept.

creche A model or painting of the scene of Christ's birth.

doctorate The degree or status of a doctor.

fertile Able to produce crops and plants easily.

pact An agreement or promise.

radium A silvery-white metal that glows in the dark.

reserve A protected area of land.

Fast Facts

The Republic of Poland is in central Europe. It is about the size of New Mexico. Most of this 120,725-square-mile (312,683-square-km) country is a flat, fertile plain.

The Vistula River is Poland's longest river. It flows 675 miles (1,086 km) from the Carpathian Mountains to the Baltic Sea.

Mount Rysy, in the High Tatras Mountains, reaches 8,199 feet (2,499 m). It is Poland's highest mountain.

The flag of Poland is made up of two horizontal bands. The white one on top symbolizes freedom. The red one below represents the blood of those who died for Poland's freedom.

The Central Plains are covered with thousands of farms that produce beets, rye, potatoes, and sugar. Many of Poland's major cities are also on the plains, including Warsaw, the capital.

Map labels: Gdansk, Szczecin, Odra River, Vistula River, Warsaw, Opole, Katowice, Kraków, Wadowice, Mount Rysy

In 2003 in Poland, 95 percent of the people were Roman Catholic and 5 percent were Eastern Orthodox, Protestant, or other religions.

Poland's main unit of currency is the zloty. It is expected that Poland will join the European Union (EU) in 2004, and the European Monetary Union (EMU) in 2007. The zloty would then be replaced by the euro.

Kraków is one of Poland's oldest and most charming cities. It is at the foothills of the Carpathian Mountains. Kraków was one of the few Polish cities that was not destroyed during World War II.

The language of Poland is Polish. Polish has thirty-two alphabet letters. That is six more than the English alphabet.

Poland will become a member of the European Union in 2004. The EU is a group of western European nations that work together on issues of money, science, and politics.

As of July 2003, there were 38,622,660 people living in Poland.

Proud to Be Polish

Frédéric Chopin (1810–1849)

Frédéric Chopin was born near Warsaw, the son of a Polish mother and French father. He was Poland's greatest composer and one of the best pianists in history. He studied at the Warsaw Lyceum and the Warsaw Conservatory. At the age of twenty-one, after finishing school, he moved to Paris. He quickly became known throughout the world. During his short career, Chopin wrote a lot of music, including fifty mazurkas, thirteen waltzes, twelve polonaises, and three sonatas. He loved his country very much and was very upset when Russia defeated Poland in the early 1800s. Chopin was a very successful musician, but his career was cut short by tuberculosis. He died in 1849 and was buried in Paris. Over 3,000 people came to his funeral.

Marie Curie (1867–1934)

Marie Sklodowska Curie is perhaps the greatest woman scientist the world ever knew. She was born in Warsaw. At that time, the nation of Poland had been divided up between Austria, Prussia, and Russia. Curie grew up feeling like a prisoner in her homeland. For many years, she studied science secretly on her own. Finally in 1891, at the age of twenty-four, she left Poland to study at the Sorbonne, in France. There she met her husband, Pierre Curie, also a scientist.

Together they discovered the element called *radium* and were awarded the Nobel Prize in Physics in 1903. Marie Curie was given a second Nobel Prize in 1911 for her work in chemistry. She was the first person ever to win two Nobel Prizes. Her work led to the use of X rays. She was the first woman to receive a *doctorate* in science and the first female professor at the Sorbonne. She and Pierre had two children, Irene and Eve. Her oldest daughter, Irene, also won a Nobel Prize in Chemistry in 1935. The Curies founded the Radium Institute, a research organization. In 1920, Marie created the Curie Foundation to help raise money for the institute. It became a major force in the fight against cancer.

Karol Wojtyla (1920–   )

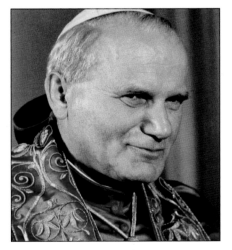

Most people know Karol Wojtyla as Pope John Paul II, the head of the Roman Catholic Church. He is the first Polish pope in history. He was born in Wadowice, near Kraków. Before he became a priest, he was a playwright and an actor. While the Nazis controlled Poland during World War II, he began studying for the priesthood. He was ordained in 1946. He taught at the University of Kraków and was made archbishop in 1963. When Poland was taken over by the Communists, he spoke out against it. He was made pope in 1978 and quickly became known all over the world. In 1981 he was shot by a terrorist. His three visits to Poland inspired his countrymen. Many people believe he is one of the reasons Communism was defeated in 1989, making Poland free. Although sometimes ill and weak, Pope John Paul still travels around the world to speak to audiences.

Find Out More

Books

Enchantment of the World: Poland by Martin Hintz. Children's Press, Connecticut, 1998.

Exploring Cultures of the World: Poland by Eleanor H. Ayer. Marshall Cavendish, New York, 1996.

Globe-Trotters Club: Poland by Sean McCollum. Carolrhoda Books, Minnesota, 1999.

Nations in Transition: Poland by Steven Otfinoski. Facts on File, New York, 1995.

Web Sites*

http://www.poland.pl/
The official website of Poland

http://www.yahooligans.com/around_the_world/countries/poland/
Links to photographs and maps of Poland

Videos

Poland: A Proud Heritage. VHS, 55 minutes. Video Visits, 1989.

*All Internet sites were available and accurate when sent to press.

Index

Page numbers for illustrations are in **boldface.**

About the Author

Sharon Gordon has written many nature and science books for young children. She has worked as an advertising copywriter and a book club editor. She is writing other books for the *Discovering Cultures* series. Sharon and her husband Bruce have three teenage children, Douglas, Katie, and Laura, and one spoiled pooch, Samantha. They live in Midland Park, New Jersey. The family especially enjoys traveling to the Outer Banks of North Carolina. After she puts her three children through college, Sharon hopes to visit the many exciting places she has come to love through her writing and research.